SUPER SIMPLE WEEKNIGHT DINNER COOKBOOK

365 Days Fast, Flavorful Dinners for Everyday Home Cooking

Bhin Tim

CONTENTS

Sweet chilli chicken bites 44

Baked BBQ chicken wings 46

BBQ chicken pizza 48

Greek chicken salad 50

Tandoori chicken drumsticks 51

Indian butter chicken 53

Pork 55

Lemon pork with mushrooms 55

Sugar and salt pork roast 57

Korean pulled pork tacos 58

Pork Verde 60

Cubano sandwiches 61

Pork piperade 62

Cherry pork chops 64

Pork chop potato dinner 65

Apple onion pork tenderloin 66

Creamy paprika pork 67

Beef 68

Beef in mushroom sauce 68

Aloha chili 70

Shepherd's pie 71

Spinach beef soup 72

Sesame beef skewers 73

Deep dish beef and bean pizza 74

Balsamic Steak salad 76

Stovetop cheeseburger pasta 78

BBQ beef and vegetables stir-fry 80

Meat loaf cups 81

Seafood 82

Baked cod and asparagus 82

Salmon with dill sauce 83

INTRODUCTION

Putting dinner on the table night after night can become a challenging task. Being the primary weekly meal planner in your family is a never-ending task that necessitates your undivided attention and effort every night. It can be exhausting at times. And most people prefer to eat outside in their busy schedule routine because they have no time to plan or cook complex meals at home after a hectic day. But only eating and working are not necessary, living a healthy life should be the main concern of every individual and one of the most effective ways to maintain a healthy lifestyle is to cook more meals at home. According to a study of over 9,000 people published in Public Health Nutrition, cooking meals at home was associated with weight loss, eating fewer calories and fat and eating more nutritious foods. So, wouldn't it be great if there was a way to make all this less difficult? So that everyone can enjoy a healthy life with these easy recipes with little effort at home.

SAUCES, DRESSINGS

ROMESCO SAUCE

Preparation Time: 5 minutes
Cooking Time: 0 minutes
Serve: 6

Ingredients:

- ½ cup raw hazelnuts
- ½ cup slivered almonds
- 1 (14.5-ounce) can diced fire roasted tomatoes, drained
- 1 (12-ounce) jar roasted red peppers, drained
- 3 garlic cloves, peeled
- 2 tablespoons red wine vinegar or sherry vinegar
- 1 teaspoon smoked paprika
- 1 teaspoon kosher salt
- ¼ cup extra-virgin olive oil, or more for a thinner texture

Directions:

1. Toast the hazelnuts in a small pan over medium heat for 5 to 8 minutes, stirring periodically. Then place them on a plate to cool.

2. While the hazelnuts cool, toast the almonds in the same pan for 3 to 4 minutes, stirring regularly, until lightly brown and aromatic. When the hazelnuts are cool enough to handle, rub them together with your hands or a kitchen towel to remove the skins.

3. Blend the nuts, tomatoes, red peppers, garlic, vinegar, paprika, salt, and oil in a high-powered blender or food processor until smooth.

4. Using a food processor to make romesco sauce

5. Serve garnished with chopped nuts and fresh parsley.

Nutritional Value (Amount per Serving):

Calories 198 kcal; Fat 20 g; Carbohydrates 4 g; Sugar 1 g; Protein 4 g

Preparation Time: 5 minutes
Cooking Time: 0 minutes
Serve: 5

Ingredients:

- 1/4 cup tahini
- 1/3 cup water
- 1 tablespoon maple syrup or honey
- 1 lemon, juiced
- 1 garlic clove, minced
- salt and pepper, to taste

Directions:

1. In a small bowl, whisk together all the ingredients.

2. Refrigerate it in an airtight jar for up to a week.

Nutritional Value (Amount per Serving):

Calories 74 kcal; Fat 6 g; Carbohydrates 5 g; Sugar 1 g; Protein 2 g

Preparation Time: 5 minutes
Cooking Time: 0 minutes
Serve: 4

Ingredients:

- 3 egg yolks
- 1 tablespoon lemon juice, or more as desired for flavor
- 1 teaspoon Dijon mustard
- 1/4 teaspoon salt
- pinch of cayenne pepper
- 1/2 cup unsalted butter or ghee, or more for a thinner consistency, melted and hot

Directions:

1. Melt the butter in a microwave (covered, since it will splatter) for about 1 minute, or until hot. You could also heat it up on the stove.

2. In a high-powered blender, combine the egg yolks, lemon juice, Dijon, salt, and cayenne pepper for 5 seconds, or until blended.

3. Slowly pour in the heated butter into the mixture while the blender is running on medium high until it's emulsified.

4. Serve the hollandaise sauce in a small bowl while it's still warm.

Nutritional Value (Amount per Serving):

Calories 249 kcal; Fat 27 g; Carbohydrates 1 g; Sugar 1 g; Protein 2 g

Preparation Time: 5 minutes
Cooking Time: 10 minutes
Serve: 8

Ingredients:

- 2 cups turkey drippings, or low-sodium chicken/turkey broth
- 2 tablespoons arrowroot powder, or more if you'd like it thicker
- 2 tablespoons butter or ghee, melted (or water for dairy-free)
- teaspoon salt and pepper, to taste

Directions:

1. When the turkey is done roasting, remove it from the pan and pour the pan drippings into a large measuring cup using a fine mesh sieve.

2. Both turkeys were drained into a cup using a sieve.

3. Allow the drippings to remain for a few minutes, until the fat separates and floats to the surface. Skim out most of the fat, leaving only 1-2 teaspoons, but keep the broth below.

4. Bring the turkey broth to a boil in a saucepan. Note: If you were unable to obtain 2 cups of turkey drippings, you can substitute with turkey or chicken broth.

5. Making turkey gravy by pouring stock into a kettle.

6. In a separate small bowl, make a slurry with the melted butter and arrowroot powder.

7. When the broth is boiling, remove it from the heat and gently whisk in the slurry until it thickens. If you want the gravy to be thicker, add another tablespoon of arrowroot powder combined with a tablespoon of water.

8. Season with salt and pepper and serve in a gravy boat. The gravy will thicken further as it cools.

Nutritional Value (Amount per Serving):

Calories 28 kcal; Fat 1g; Carbohydrates 4 g; Sugar 1 g; Protein 2 g

Preparation Time: 5 minutes
Cooking Time: 0 minutes
Serve: 8

Ingredients:

- 1/3 cup red wine vinegar
- 1 lemon, juiced
- 1 tsp Dijon Mustard
- 2 garlic cloves, minced
- 1/2 tsp dried oregano
- 1/4 tsp salt
- 1/4 tsp black pepper
- 1/2 cup olive oil

Directions:

1. In a mixing bowl, whisk together all the ingredients except the olive oil.

2. Slowly drizzle in the olive oil, whisking rapidly as you pour, until the dressing is emulsified.

Nutritional Value (Amount per Serving):

Calories 123.5 kcal; Fat 13.6g; Carbohydrates 0.5 g; Sugar 0.2g; Protein 0.1 g

Preparation Time: 5 minutes
Cooking Time: 0 minutes
Serve: 12

Ingredients:

- 1 cup mayonnaise
- 1 tbsp honey or maple syrup, (or more if desired)
- 2 tbsp apple cider vinegar
- 1 tsp celery seeds
- 1/4 tsp salt
- 1/4 tsp pepper

Directions:

1. In a small bowl, whisk together the mayonnaise, honey, apple cider vinegar, salt, pepper, and celery seeds. Add another tablespoon of honey if you want the dressing to be sweeter.

2. Toss the cabbage and carrots with a little of the dressing. Slowly drizzle in extra dressing until you reach the desired consistency.

3. Serve and have fun!

Nutritional Value (Amount per Serving):

Calories 134 kcal; Fat 14 g; Carbohydrates 2 g; Sugar 2 g; Protein 1 g

Preparation Time: 5 minutes
Cooking Time: 15 minutes
Serve: 8
Ingredients:

- 4 cups (12oz package) fresh or frozen cranberries
- 1/2 cup honey or maple syrup, or more as desired
- 1/2 cup orange juice
- 1/2 cup water
- orange zest, optional

Directions:

1. Heat the water, orange juice, and honey in a saucepan over medium-high heat. Bring the water to a boil.

2. Add the cranberries and whisk everything together.

3. Cranberries simmering in a pot for cranberry sauce

4. Bring the mixture back to a boil, then lower to a low heat. Allow it to simmer for 5-10 minutes, stirring regularly. The cranberries will burst (which is exactly what you want) and the sauce will thicken.

5. A pot with cranberry sauce on the stove.

6. Turn off the heat and let aside for 15 minutes to cool. Then pour it into a container and place it in the refrigerator to cold and thicken.

Nutritional Value (Amount per Serving):

Calories 94 kcal; Fat 1g; Carbohydrates 25 g; Sugar 21 g; Protein 1 g

Preparation Time: 10 minutes
Cooking Time: 10 minutes
Serve: 8

Ingredients:

- 1 1/2 cups Greek yogurt
- 1 medium cucumber, peeled and grated
- 2 tablespoon fresh dill, chopped
- 2 cloves garlic, minced
- 2 tablespoon olive oil
- 1 tablespoon fresh lemon juice
- 1/2 teaspoon salt

Directions:

1. Drain the grated cucumber by pushing it through a fine mesh strainer set over a basin. Alternatively, use a nut milk bag or cheesecloth to carefully squeeze out all the moisture.

2. In a large mixing basin, blend all the ingredients until well incorporated.

3. Allow the mixture to stand for a few minutes to allow the flavors to mingle. Taste to determine if any additional herbs, lemon juice, or salt are required.

4. Serve immediately or store in the fridge for up to 4 days.

Nutritional Value (Amount per Serving):

Calories 59 kcal; Fat 4 g; Carbohydrates 3 g; Sugar 2 g; Protein 4 g

Preparation Time: 5 minutes
Cooking Time: 0 minutes
Serve: 6

Ingredients:

- 1/3 cup olive oil
- 3 limes, juiced
- 1/2 cup fresh cilantro, chopped
- 4 garlic cloves, minced
- 1 teaspoon cumin powder
- 1/2 teaspoon chili powder
- salt and pepper, to taste

Directions:

1. In a small mixing dish, combine all the marinade ingredients.

2. Pour the marinade over the meat, making sure both sides are well coated.

3. Before grilling, cover and marinate for 1-4 hours in the refrigerator.

Nutritional Value (Amount per Serving):

Calories 121 kcal; Fat 12 g; Carbohydrates 4 g; Sugar 1 g; Protein 1 g

Preparation Time: 5 minutes
Cooking Time: 0 minutes
Serve: 1

Ingredients:

- 1 tbsp chili powder
- 1 tsp ground cumin
- 1 tsp garlic powder
- 1/2 tsp paprika (or smoked paprika)
- 1/2 tsp oregano
- 1/2 tsp salt
- 1/4 tsp black pepper
- pinch of red pepper flakes or cayenne pepper, optional

Directions:

1. In a mixing dish, combine all the spices. Use right away or keep in an airtight container.

Nutritional Value (Amount per Serving):

Calories 46 kcal; Fat 1 g; Carbohydrates 8 g; Sugar 0 g; Protein 2 g

CAULIFLOWER TIKKA MASALA WITH CHICKPEAS

Preparation Time: 20minutes
Cooking Time: 0 minutes
Serve: 4

Ingredients:

- 1 tablespoon coconut or canola oil
- 4 cups cauliflower florets
- ¼ teaspoon salt
- ¼ cup water
- 1 (15 ounce) can chickpeas, rinsed
- 1 1/2 cups tikka masala sauce (see Tip)
- 2 tablespoons butter
- Fresh cilantro for garnish

Directions:

1. In a large skillet over medium-high heat, heat the oil. Cook, tossing occasionally, until the cauliflower is gently browned, about 2 minutes. Cook, covered, for 3 to 5 minutes, or until the cauliflower is soft. Cook, tossing periodically, until the chickpeas and sauce are heated, 1 to 2 minutes. Remove from the heat and add the butter. If desired, garnish with cilantro.

Nutritional Value (Amount per Serving):

Calories 268 kcal; Fat 16.9 g; Carbohydrates 26.3 g; Sugar 4.1 g; Protein 7.8 g

Preparation Time: 15minutes
Cooking Time: 5 minutes
Serve: 4

Ingredients:

- 8 ounces cavatappi or rotini, preferably whole wheat
- 2 tablespoons extra-virgin olive oil
- ½ cup halved and sliced onion
- 2 cups chopped broccoli
- ½ teaspoon salt
- ¼ teaspoon crushed red pepper
- ½ cup mascarpone cheese (3 ounces)
- ¼ cup low-fat plain Greek yogurt
- 1 teaspoon garlic powder
- Grated Parmesan cheese (Optional)

Directions:

1. Bring a big pot of water to a boil over high heat. Cook the pasta according to the package directions. 1/2 cup of the cooking water should be set aside. Return the spaghetti to the pot after draining.

2. Meanwhile, in a large skillet over medium-high heat, heat the oil. Cook, stirring constantly, for 1 minute. Cook, stirring constantly, until the broccoli, salt, and crushed red pepper are tender, about 3 minutes more. Turn off the heat.

3. In a small mixing dish, combine the mascarpone, yoghurt, garlic powder, and conserved pasta water. Combine with the broccoli mixture and add to the pasta. To coat, thoroughly mix everything together. Allow for a 5-minute rest before serving. If preferred, top with Parmesan cheese.

Nutritional Value (Amount per Serving):

Calories 562 kcal; Fat 36 g; Carbohydrates 51 g; Sugar 3 g; Protein 16 g

Preparation Time: 15minutes
Cooking Time: 0 minutes
Serve: 1

Ingredients:

- 2 cups water
- ½ (3 ounce) package rice-noodle soup mix, such as Thai Kitchen Garlic & Vegetable
- 1 large egg
- 1 cup baby spinach
- 1 scallion, sliced

Directions:

1. In a small saucepan, heat water to a boil. Half of the seasoning packet should be added at this point (discard the remainder or reserve for another use). Cook for 3 minutes, or until noodles are soft. Maintain a simmer by lowering the heat.

2. In a small mixing dish, whisk together the egg. Stir constantly as you slowly pour the egg into the cooking broth. Fold in the spinach for 30 seconds, or until it is barely wilted. Sprinkle with scallions and transfer to a bowl.

Nutritional Value (Amount per Serving):

Calories 258 kcal; Fat 7.3 g; Carbohydrates 36.5 g; Sugar 2.5 g; Protein 10.9 g

Preparation Time: 15minutes
Cooking Time: 15 minutes
Serve: 4

Ingredients:

- 3 tablespoons extra-virgin olive oil
- 1 ½ teaspoons ground cumin, divided
- 1 teaspoon ground coriander
- ½ teaspoon garlic powder
- ½ teaspoon smoked paprika
- ½ teaspoon chipotle chile powder
- ½ teaspoon salt plus 1/8 teaspoon, divided
- 1-pound portobello mushrooms, stemmed, gills removed, halved, and sliced (see Tip)
- 1 medium red onion, halved and sliced
- ½ cup low-fat plain Greek yogurt
- 2 tablespoons tahini
- 1 tablespoon lemon juice
- 4 pitas, warmed
- 1 cup chopped romaine lettuce
- 1 cup chopped tomatoes
- ½ cup cilantro leaves

Directions:

1. Preheat the oven to 425°F. In a large mixing bowl, combine the oil, cumin, coriander, garlic powder, smoked paprika, chile powder, and 1/2 teaspoon salt. Stir in the mushrooms and onion until fully coated. Transfer to a large rimmed baking sheet and roast, stirring once or twice, for 20 minutes, or until the veggies are soft.

2. Meanwhile, in a separate dish, combine the yoghurt, tahini, lemon juice, and the remaining 1/2 teaspoon cumin and 1/8 teaspoon salt.

3. Spread the yoghurt sauce over the pitas, then top with the mushroom mixture, lettuce, tomatoes, and cilantro.

Nutritional Value (Amount per Serving):

Calories 281 kcal; Fat 15.9 g; Carbohydrates 28.7 g; Sugar 7.4 g; Protein 10.1 g

Preparation Time: 10minutes
Cooking Time: 5 minutes
Serve: 6

Ingredients:

- 4 Japanese eggplants (about 1 1/2 pounds)
- 5 tablespoons canola oil or peanut oil, divided
- 2 tablespoons hoisin sauce
- 2 tablespoons reduced-sodium soy sauce
- 1 tablespoon plum sauce
- 2 jalapeño peppers, cut into thin rings
- 1 small yellow onion, sliced into 1/4-inch wedges
- 2 teaspoons minced garlic
- 1 teaspoon minced fresh ginger
- 1 cup packed fresh basil leaves

Directions:

1. Cut the eggplants lengthwise into quarters, then into 2-inch slices. In a large cast-iron skillet, heat 2 tablespoons oil over high heat. Cook, tossing occasionally, until half of the eggplant is soft and browned in spots, 4 to 5 minutes. Transfer to a large mixing bowl. Repeat with the remaining eggplant and 2 tablespoons oil. Set aside and cover the eggplant to keep it warm.

2. Meanwhile, in a small bowl, combine the hoisin, soy sauce, and plum sauce. Place aside.

3. In the skillet, heat the remaining 1 tablespoon oil over high heat. Cook, turning frequently, until the jalapenos and onion are slightly softened, 4 to 5 minutes. Cook, stirring frequently, until the garlic and ginger are cooked and aromatic, 30 seconds to 1 minute.Stir in the sauce after adding the onion mixture and basil to the eggplant. Serve right away.

Nutritional Value (Amount per Serving):

Calories 161 kcal; Fat 12.2 g; Carbohydrates 12.6 g; Sugar 1.5 g; Protein 2.3 g

Preparation Time: 30 minutes
Cooking Time: 18 minutes
Serve: 3

Ingredients:

Rice:

- 3 cups water
- 1 cup long-grain brown rice
- ½ teaspoon salt

Dressing:

- 1 lime, juiced
- 2 tablespoons olive oil
- 1 tablespoon sesame oil
- 1 tablespoon dried Thai basil
- 1 teaspoon minced hot Chile pepper

Vegetables:

- 2 tablespoons sesame seeds
- ½ (8 ounce) package snow peas
- 1 cup cooked chickpeas, drained
- ½ (16 ounce) package firm tofu, cut into strips
- 16 baby corn, cut into bite-sized pieces
- 1 cup grated carrots
- 1 small green bell pepper, diced
- 2 green onions, cut on the diagonal
- 2 tablespoons chopped fresh cilantro

Directions:

1. In a pressure cooker, combine water, brown rice, and salt. Close and secure the lid; bring to high pressure as directed by the manufacturer. Cooking time is 10 minutes. Release the pressure naturally, as directed by the manufacturer. Remove any excess water from the rice and place it in a large mixing basin.

2. To prepare the dressing, combine lime juice, olive oil, sesame oil, Thai basil, and chilli pepper in a small bowl.

3. Toast sesame seeds in a nonstick skillet over medium-low heat, stirring periodically, for 5 minutes, or until evenly toasted and aromatic. Transfer to a mixing basin.

4. In the same skillet, cook and stir snow peas until brilliant green, 3 to 5 minutes. Remove from the heat and cool it.

5. Over the brown rice, arrange the snow peas, chickpeas, tofu, baby corn, carrots, and green bell pepper. Drizzle the dressing over the entire bowl and toss to combine. Top with toasted sesame seeds. Garnish with green onions and cilantro if desired.

Nutritional Value (Amount per Serving):

Calories 583 kcal; Fat 22.6 g; Carbohydrates 80.5 g; Sugar 6.9 g; Protein 18 g

Preparation Time: 15minutes
Cooking Time: 20 minutes
Serve: 4
Ingredients:

- 1 (16 ounce) can black beans, drained and rinsed
- ½ green bell pepper, cut into 2-inch pieces
- ½ onion, cut into wedges
- 3 cloves garlic, peeled
- 1 egg
- 1 tablespoon chili powder
- 1 tablespoon cumin
- 1 teaspoon Thai chili sauce or hot sauce
- ½ cup bread crumbs

Directions:

1. Preheat an outside grill to high heat and lightly oil a layer of aluminum foil if grilling. If baking, preheat the oven to 375°F (190°C) and gently oil a baking sheet.

2. Mash black beans with a fork in a medium bowl until thick and pasty.

3. Finely chop the bell pepper, onion, and garlic in a food processor. Then fold in the mashed beans.

4. In a small mixing dish, combine the egg, chili powder, cumin, and chili sauce.

5. Combine the egg mixture and the mashed beans in a mixing bowl. Mix in the bread crumbs until the mixture is sticky and cohesive. Make four patties out of the mixture.

6. Place patties on foil and grill for 8 minutes on each side if grilling. If baking, arrange patties on a baking sheet and bake for about 15 minutes.

Nutritional Value (Amount per Serving):

Calories 198.4 kcal; Fat 3 g; Carbohydrates 33.1 g; Sugar 2.1 g; Protein 11.2 g

Preparation Time: 20 minutes
Cooking Time: 40 minutes
Serve: 2

Ingredients:

- 1 cup water
- ½ cup uncooked Arborio rice
- 2 green bell peppers, halved and seeded
- 1 tablespoon olive oil
- 2 green onions, thinly sliced
- 1 teaspoon dried basil
- 1 teaspoon Italian seasoning
- 1 teaspoon salt
- 1 pinch ground black pepper
- 1 tomato, diced
- ½ cup crumbled feta cheese

Directions:

1. Preheat the oven to 400°F (200 degrees C). Grease a baking sheet lightly.

2. Bring water to a boil in a medium saucepan. Add the rice and mix well. Reduce the heat to low, cover, and leave to simmer for 20 minutes. Set aside after removing from the heat.

3. Place the peppers, cut side down, on a baking sheet lined with parchment paper. Roast for 25 to 30 minutes, or until soft and the skin begins to brown, in a preheated oven.

4. Heat the oil in a medium skillet over medium-high heat while the peppers roast. Cook for 2 to 3 minutes in oil with the onions, basil, Italian seasoning, salt, and pepper. Cook for 5 minutes after adding the tomato. Stir in the cooked rice until it is heated

through. Remove from the heat, stir in the feta cheese, and ladle the marmalade on top.

5. Return to the oven for a further 5 minutes. Serve right away.

Nutritional Value (Amount per Serving):

Calories 384.5 kcal; Fat 15.2 g; Carbohydrates 52.6 g; Sugar 6.4 g; Protein 10.8 g

Preparation Time: 30 minutes
Cooking Time: 20 minutes
Serve: 4

Ingredients:

- ¼ cup mayonnaise
- 3 cloves garlic, minced
- 1 tablespoon lemon juice
- ⅛ cup olive oil
- 1 cup sliced red bell peppers
- 1 small zucchini, sliced
- 1 red onion, sliced
- 1 small yellow squash, sliced
- 2 (4-x6-inch) focaccia bread pieces, split horizontally
- ½ cup crumbled feta cheese

Directions:

1. Combine the mayonnaise, minced garlic, and lemon juice in a mixing bowl. Refrigerate until ready to use.

2. Preheat the grill to high.

3. Brush each side of the vegetables with olive oil. Using a brush, coat the grate with oil. Place the bell peppers and zucchini closest to the centre of the grill, followed by the onion and squash pieces. Cook for 3 minutes, then flip and cook for another 3 minutes. The peppers can take a little longer. Set aside after removing from the grill.

4. Spread some of the mayonnaise mixture on each sliced side of the bread and top with feta cheese. Place the cheese side up on the grill and cover with the lid for 2 to 3 minutes. This will warm the bread and melt the cheese slightly.

5. Keep a close eye on the bottoms so they don't burn. Remove from the grill and top with veggies. As open-faced grilled sandwiches, serve.

Nutritional Value (Amount per Serving):

Calories 392.9 kcal; Fat 23.8 g; Carbohydrates 36.5 g; Sugar 4.7 g; Protein 9.2 g

Preparation Time: 10 minutes
Cooking Time: 30 minutes
Serve: 8
Ingredients:

- 2 cups red lentils
- 1 large onion, diced
- 1 tablespoon vegetable oil
- 2 tablespoons curry paste
- 1 tablespoon curry powder
- 1 teaspoon ground turmeric
- 1 teaspoon ground cumin
- 1 teaspoon chili powder
- 1 teaspoon salt
- 1 teaspoon white sugar
- 1 teaspoon minced garlic
- 1 teaspoon minced fresh ginger
- 1 (14.25 ounce) can tomato puree

Directions:

1. Wash the lentils in cold water until they are clear. Put lentils in a pot with enough water to cover; bring to a boil, cover, decrease heat to medium-low, and simmer, adding water as required to keep covered, for 15 to 20 minutes, or until cooked. Drain.

2. In a large skillet over medium heat, heat vegetable oil; sauté and stir onions in hot oil until caramelized, about 20 minutes.

3. In a large mixing bowl, combine the curry paste, curry powder, turmeric, cumin, chilli powder, salt, sugar, garlic, and ginger; stir into the onions. Increase the heat to high and cook, stirring constantly, for 1 to 2 minutes, or until aromatic.

4. Stir in the tomato puree, then remove from the heat and fold into the lentils

Nutritional Value (Amount per Serving):

Calories 191.7 kcal; Fat 2.6 g; Carbohydrates 32.5 g; Sugar 6.6 g; Protein 12.1 g

ONE PAN GARLIC ROASTED CHICKEN AND BABY POTATOES

Preparation Time: 10 minutes
Cooking Time: 1 hour and 25 minutes
Serve: 4 to 6
Ingredients:

- 5 to 6 chicken thighs, bone-in and skin on (2 lbs. total)
- 15-20 baby potatoes, halved
- ½ onion, quartered
- 4 cloves garlic, minced
- 2 to 3 tablespoons olive oil
- 2 teaspoons salt (or to taste)
- ½ teaspoon ground black pepper (or to taste)
- 1 tablespoon dried rosemary

Directions:

1. Preheat the oven to 350°F.

2. Combine the chicken, potatoes, carrots, onion, garlic, and olive oil in a large roasting pan or casserole dish. Toss to coat and season with salt and pepper.

3. Place the chicken in the middle of the potatoes. Then, on top of the chicken and vegetables, sprinkle with dried rosemary.

4. Cook for 1 hour and 25 minutes, or until the skin is crispy and golden brown and the potatoes are tender when probed with a fork.

5. Turn the broiler to high and broil for 3-4 minutes, or until the skin is crisp and browned. Keep a tight eye on the broiler since items can burn quickly.

6. Serve immediately after removing from the oven.

Nutritional Value (Amount per Serving):

Calories 432 kcal; Fat 12.2 g; Carbohydrates 46.4 g; Sugar 3.9 g; Protein 34.4 g

Preparation Time: 10 minutes
Cooking Time: 25 minutes
Serve: 2

Ingredients:

- 2 tablespoons olive oil
- lemon juice from half a lemon
- 2 clove garlic, pressed or minced
- 2 tablespoons fresh parsley, chopped
- 1 tablespoon dried oregano
- 1 teaspoon dried mint (or dill)
- 1 teaspoon paprika (optional)
- ½ teaspoon salt
- ½ teaspoon ground black pepper
- 2 chicken breasts, boneless and skinless

Directions:

1. Combine the olive oil, lemon juice, garlic, parsley, oregano, dill, paprika, salt, and pepper in a medium mixing bowl.

2. Pour the marinade over the chicken breasts in a large shallow bowl. Toss the chicken in the marinade to coat it completely.

3. Cover the bowl with plastic wrap and place it in the refrigerator for 1 hour to marinate the chicken.

4. Preheat the oven to 450 degrees Fahrenheit. Place the chicken on a quarter sheet baking pan and bake for 20-25 minutes, or until the chicken is no longer pink on the inside and the internal temperature reaches 165 degrees Fahrenheit in the thickest portion of the chicken breast (as read on a meat thermometer).

5. Allow the chicken to rest for 5 minutes after removing it from the oven. Serve with Greek salad, pita bread, rice pilaf, and Greek lemon roasted potatoes. Don't forget about the tzatziki sauce.

Nutritional Value (Amount per Serving):

Calories 231 kcal; Fat 10.7 g; Carbohydrates 2.1 g; Sugar 0.4 g; Protein 30.9 g

Preparation Time: 5 minutes
Cooking Time: 8 minutes
Serve: 2-4

Ingredients:

- 2 tablespoons vegetable oil
- ½ cup onions, finely chopped
- 2 tablespoons garlic, minced
- 1 boneless and skinless chicken breast, cooked and cut into ½-inch cubes
- ⅓ cup mushrooms, finely chopped
- 3 cups long grain white rice, cooked (warm or cold)
- ½ cup peas, frozen
- 2 tablespoons yellow curry powder
- 2 tablespoons soy sauce
- 1 teaspoon salt
- ½ teaspoon ground black pepper
- 1 tablespoon fresh parsley, finely chopped (for garnish)

Directions:

1. In a large skillet, heat the oil over medium high heat for 2 minutes, or until it begins to sizzle and shimmer. Sauté the onions and garlic for 2 minutes, or until aromatic. (Optional: Stir in 1 or 2 beaten eggs and cook until frothy.)

2. Mix in the diced chicken and mushrooms. Stir fry for 1 minute more to mix. Combine precooked rice and frozen peas in a mixing bowl. Stir fry for 2 minutes with a spatula to combine everything.

3. Season with curry powder, soy sauce, salt, and pepper to taste. Stir for 2 minutes more to properly distribute the seasonings.

4. Garnish with chopped parsley and serve warm on a platter.

Nutritional Value (Amount per Serving):

Calories 368 kcal; Fat 9.5 g; Carbohydrates 48.6 g; Sugar 2.4 g; Protein 21.3 g

Preparation Time: 10 minutes
Cooking Time: 15 minutes
Serve: 3-4

Ingredients:

For the chicken:

- 1 + ½ lbs. chicken breasts (about 2-3 breasts), boneless and skinless and cut into 1-inch pieces
- 1 tablespoon soy sauce
- ½ tablespoon Chinese cooking wine
- 1 teaspoon apple cider vinegar
- 1 tablespoon cornstarch

For the sauce:

- 2 tablespoons vegetable oil
- ¼ cup sugar
- ½ cup lemon juice, freshly squeezed
- 1 teaspoon lemon zest, grated
- 2 tablespoons liquid honey
- 1 teaspoon soy sauce
- 2 tablespoons cornstarch
- ⅓ cup water
- 2 teaspoons white sesame seeds (for garnish)
- 1 teaspoon green onions, finely chopped (for garnish)
- ½ lemon, thinly sliced (for garnish)

Directions:

1. Combine the chicken, soy sauce, cooking wine, vinegar, and cornstarch in a medium mixing bowl. Combine all the ingredients in a mixing bowl until the chicken is completely coated. Squeeze out all the air from the Ziploc bag containing the chicken and marinade. Refrigerate the bag for at least 1 hour to allow it to marinade. Allow it to marinade for a longer period if you have the time.

2. Heat the oil in a big nonstick frying pan or wok for 2 minutes over medium high heat, until it sizzles and shimmers. Add the chicken to the frying pan and continue to stir fry for 7-10 minutes, or until the chicken is no longer pink on the inside.

3. For a minute, whisk in the sugar to coat the chicken. The melted sugar will caramelize the chicken, turning it brown. Combine the lemon juice, lemon zest, honey, and soy sauce in a mixing bowl. To coat the chicken, put all the ingredients in a large mixing bowl.

4. Whisk together the water and cornstarch in a small mixing dish. Pour in the cornstarch mixture and stir vigorously until the sauce thickens and achieves a smooth consistency. Coat the chicken evenly with the mixture. Top with sesame seeds and chopped green onions.

5. Garnish with more sesame seeds and lemon slices and serve over steaming rice.

Nutritional Value (Amount per Serving):

Calories 393 kcal; Fat 12.2 g; Carbohydrates 32.1 g; Sugar 23 g; Protein 39.2 g

Preparation Time: 25 minutes
Cooking Time: 30 minutes
Serve: 3-4

Ingredients:

- 1 lb. chicken breasts, boneless and skinless
- 1 tablespoon salt
- 1 teaspoon ground black pepper
- 1 teaspoon paprika
- ¼ cup all-purpose flour
- 2 eggs, beaten
- 2 cups breadcrumbs
- cooking oil spray
- ½ cup sweet chili sauce, homemade or store-bought
- 1 tablespoon green onions, finely chopped (for garnish)
- 1 teaspoon white sesame seeds (for garnish)

For homemade sweet chili sauce:

- ¼ cup rice vinegar
- 1 tablespoon fish sauce (or soy sauce)
- 2 tablespoons brown sugar
- 2 tablespoons sambal oelek (or chili garlic sauce)
- 1 teaspoon cornstarch (or flour)
- 2 tablespoons water

Directions:

1. Preheat the oven to 375 degrees Fahrenheit.

2. Dry the chicken breasts entirely with a paper towel before cutting them into 1-inch cubes. Season with salt, pepper, and paprika in a medium mixing bowl. Allow for at least 5 minutes.

3. Combine flour and cubed chicken in a big Ziploc bag. Seal the bag and shake vigorously to coat.

4. Make a shallow plate with beaten eggs and another with breadcrumbs. Dip the chicken, one at a time, into the egg wash,

coating it evenly. Then coat completely with breadcrumbs. To adhere and properly coat each piece, gently squeeze crumbs into it. The flour adheres to the chicken, the egg wash adheres to the flour, and the breadcrumbs adhere to the egg wash.

5. Place the breaded chicken on a large half-sheet baking pan that has been lined with parchment paper or a silicone mat. Coat the chicken in frying spray. During baking, this aids in the formation of a crispy crust on the outside.

6. Bake the chicken for 25 to 30 minutes, or until thoroughly done. The chicken's internal temperature should be 165°F.

7. Add the sweet chilli sauce to the cooked chicken in a large mixing bowl (or if making homemade sweet chilli sauce, add the chicken into the saucepan after the sauce has been cooked and thickened). To coat evenly, toss lightly and thoroughly. Sesame seeds and green onions should be sprinkled on top.

8. To prepare homemade sweet chilli sauce (rather than store-bought), combine vinegar, fish sauce, brown sugar, sambal oelek, cornstarch, and water in a medium mixing basin. Whisk until the cornstarch and sugar are dissolved.

9. Heat the sauce in a small saucepan over medium heat for 3-4 minutes. Stir until the mixture has thickened to the desired consistency.

Nutritional Value (Amount per Serving):

Calories 483 kcal; Fat 12.4 g; Carbohydrates 52.7 g; Sugar 8.1 g; Protein 37.8 g

Preparation Time: 10 minutes
Cooking Time: 52 minutes
Serve: 4-6

Ingredients:

- 2 lbs. chicken wings
- 1 tablespoon vegetable oil
- 1 tablespoon paprika
- 1 tablespoon Italian seasoning (optional)
- ½ tablespoon garlic powder
- 1 tablespoon salt
- 1 tablespoon ground black pepper
- 1 tablespoon white sesame seeds (for garnish)

For the BBQ Sauce:

- ⅓ cup tomato paste (or ketchup)
- ½ tablespoon soy sauce
- ½ tablespoon vinegar
- 2 tablespoons honey (or maple syrup)

Directions:

1. Before seasoning the chicken wings, pat them dry entirely with a paper towel. Combine the chicken wings, vegetable oil, Italian seasoning (if using), garlic powder, paprika, salt, and pepper in a ziploc bag. Seal the bag tightly after pressing the air out. Place the wings in the fridge to marinate for at least 30 minutes after applying the seasoning.

2. Preheat the oven to 400 degrees Fahrenheit. Place the wings on a wire rack on a quarter sheet baking pan and bake for 40 minutes, flipping halfway through.

3. In a separate bowl, whisk together tomato paste, soy sauce, vinegar, and honey to make the BBQ sauce. Refrigerate the sauce mixture for 15 minutes or overnight.

4. Remove the chicken from the oven and generously coat each wing with BBQ sauce. Return to the oven for another 5 minutes. Bake for another 5 minutes after flipping the wings and applying more BBQ sauce to the other side. The chicken's internal temperature should be 165 degrees Fahrenheit.

5. Turn the broiler to high and broil the wings for an additional 2-3 minutes to brown and crisp the skin. Keep an eye on the broiler to prevent the wings from burning.

6. Pour the remaining BBQ sauce over the wings in a large mixing bowl. To coat, toss everything together. Serve immediately, topped with sesame seeds.

Nutritional Value (Amount per Serving):

Calories 99 kcal; Fat 3.3 g; Carbohydrates 4.2 g; Sugar 2.9 g; Protein 13 g

Preparation Time: 10 minutes
Cooking Time: 15 minutes
Serve: 3

Ingredients:

- 1 cup cooked chicken breast, shredded (approximately one chicken breast)
- ¼ cup + 3 tablespoons BBQ sauce, divided
- 10 oz. pizza dough, homemade or store-bought
- 1 tablespoon cornmeal
- 1 tablespoon olive oil
- 4 oz. fresh mozzarella cheese
- ¼ cup red onion, thinly sliced
- ¼ cup cheddar cheese, grated
- 1 scallion, thinly sliced (for garnish)
- ¼ cup fresh cilantro (for garnish)
- ¼ to ½ cup micro greens (optional, for garnish)
- 1 lime, cut into wedges

Directions:

1. Preheat the oven to 450 degrees Fahrenheit. When the oven is hot, set the rimmed quarter sheet baking pan in it for at least 20 minutes.

2. Toss the chicken breast in 14 cup BBQ sauce in a shallow bowl. Place aside.

3. Roll out pizza dough to desired thickness on a lightly floured surface (remember that the cook time is based on dough that is about 14-inch thick). With a fork, prick the dough all over.

4. Remove the baking sheet from the oven and equally sprinkle with cornmeal. Bake for 7 minutes after transferring the pizza dough to a baking sheet and brushing it with olive oil.

5. Spread the remaining BBQ sauce on top of the pizza dough, leaving a 12-inch border around the perimeter. On top, layer mozzarella, chicken, red onion, and cheddar cheese.

6. Bake for another 8 minutes. Allow to cool somewhat before topping with scallions, cilantro, and micro greens (if using). With lime wedges on the side, serve.

Nutritional Value (Amount per Serving):

Calories 453 kcal; Fat 11 g; Carbohydrates 47.1 g; Sugar 17.4 g; Protein 39.2 g

Preparation Time: 5 minutes
Cooking Time: 0 minutes
Serve: 4

Ingredients:

- 1 cooked chicken breast, sliced
- 3 cups romaine lettuce
- 1 cup grape tomatoes, halved
- 2 Persian cucumbers, halved and sliced
- ½ cup red onion, diced
- ½ cup kalamata olives, pitted
- ⅓ cup feta cheese, crumbled
- ¼ cup Greek salad dressing
- 3 tablespoons olive oil
- juice from ½ lemon
- ¼ teaspoon dried oregano
- ¼ teaspoon salt (or to taste)
- ¼ teaspoon ground black pepper (or to taste)

Directions:

1. Combine the salad ingredients, including the chicken, romaine lettuce, tomatoes, cucumbers, red onion, cucumber, olives, and feta cheese, in a large serving bowl.

2. In a small mixing bowl, whisk together olive oil, lemon juice, oregano, salt, and pepper to make the Greek salad dressing.

3. Toss the salad with the dressing to mix. If desired, season with additional salt and pepper.

Nutritional Value (Amount per Serving):

Calories 274 kcal; Fat 17.2 g; Carbohydrates 13.7 g; Sugar 16 g; Protein 19.3 g

Preparation Time: 15 minutes
Cooking Time: 45 minutes
Serve: 10

Ingredients:

- 3 lb. chicken drumsticks (about 10 pieces)
- 1 teaspoon salt
- ½ teaspoon ground black pepper
- 1 teaspoon garlic powder
- 1 teaspoon ginger root powder
- 1 teaspoon ground turmeric
- 1 teaspoon ground cumin
- 1 teaspoon garam masala
- 1 teaspoon paprika (for colouring)
- 1 tablespoon olive oil
- 3 tablespoons lemon juice (from 1 freshly squeezed lemon)
- 1 cup plain Greek yogurt
- 1 teaspoon fresh cilantro, finely chopped (for garnish)

Directions:

1. Before seasoning the chicken drumsticks, blot them dry completely with a paper towel. With a knife, make 2-3 shallow slashes, approximately 14-inch deep, on each drumstick. This allows the chicken to absorb up all the spices.

2. Combine salt, pepper, garlic powder, ginger root powder, turmeric, cumin, garam masala, and paprika in a small mixing bowl. With a spoon, combine all the ingredients until they are uniformly distributed. Rub the spice all over the chicken, including in between the cuts, to coat evenly.

3. Put the chicken drumsticks in a zip-top bag. Stir in all the wet ingredients, including the oil, lemon juice, and yoghurt. Seal the bag tightly after pressing the air out. To coat the chicken

drumsticks, ress the marinade around them. Place the bag in the refrigerator for at least 1 hour, and up to overnight.

4. The chicken can be cooked in the oven, on the stovetop, or on the grill.

5. To bake in the oven, follow these steps: Preheat the oven to 400 degrees Fahrenheit. Place the marinated chicken drumsticks on a large half-sheet baking pan and bake for 40-45 minutes, or until the skin is crispy and the internal temperature of the chicken reaches 165 degrees Fahrenheit. Halfway through baking, turn the pan over. Turn the broiler to high and cook for 5 minutes more, or until beautifully blackened.

6. 1 tablespoon cooking oil in a large cast-iron skillet or fry pan over medium-high heat for 2 minutes, or until the hot oil sizzles and shimmers. Cook the drumsticks in batches for 6-8 minutes per side, or until cooked through and beautifully browned. The chicken's internal temperature should be 165 degrees Fahrenheit.

7. Preheat the grill for at least 5 minutes on high heat. Place the chicken drumsticks on the grill and cook for 3-4 minutes on each side, or until well browned and the internal temperature of the chicken reaches 165 degrees Fahrenheit. To avoid overcooking, flip the pan every now and then.

8. Allow 5 minutes for the drumsticks to rest. Drizzle with more lemon juice and top with cilantro.

Nutritional Value (Amount per Serving):

Calories 197 kcal; Fat 7.8 g; Carbohydrates 2.2 g; Sugar 1.3 g; Protein 28 g

Preparation Time: 15 minutes
Cooking Time: 30 minutes
Serve: 4-6

Ingredients:

Marinade:

- 1 + ½ lb. boneless and skinless chicken thighs or breast (about 2 chicken breasts or 4-5 thighs), cut into 1-inch cubes
- ½ cup yogurt
- 3 cloves garlic, minced
- 1 tablespoon ginger, grated
- 1 teaspoon chilli powder or red pepper powder
- ¼ teaspoon paprika
- 1 teaspoon garam masala
- ½ teaspoon salt
- ½ teaspoon pepper

Butter Chicken Sauce:

- 1 tablespoon vegetable oil
- 2 tablespoons unsalted butter
- 1 + ½ teaspoons coriander seeds
- 1 + ½ teaspoons cumin seeds
- 1 medium onion, chopped
- 1 teaspoon turmeric
- 3 cloves garlic, minced
- 1 tablespoon ginger, grated
- ½ tablespoon garam masala (or more to taste)
- 1 teaspoon chilli powder or red pepper powder
- 1 (16 oz.) can of tomato puree
- ½ cup water
- ½ cup heavy cream (35% or whipping cream)
- ½ teaspoon dried fenugreek leaves
- salt and pepper, to taste
- cilantro or parsley, chopped (for garnish)

Directions:

1. In a medium mixing bowl, combine the chicken with the marinade ingredients: yoghurt, garlic, ginger, chilli powder, salt, and pepper. Allow the chicken to marinate in the bowl for 1-2 hours or overnight in the refrigerator.

2. Preheat the oven to 475 degrees Fahrenheit. Cook the chicken on the middle rack for 10 minutes. Preheat the broiler to high and place the chicken on the top rack. Char the top of the chicken for 2-3 minutes, or until it begins to brown or burn slightly. Remove the chicken from the oven.

3. Heat the oil in a big frying pan over medium-high heat. Melt the butter in the pan. Cook for 30 seconds after adding the coriander and cumin. Cook until the onion, turmeric, garlic, and ginger are transparent.Stir in the garam masala, chilli powder, and paprika until evenly coated, and simmer for 40 seconds. Bring the sauce to a simmer with the tomato puree and water.

4. Puree the sauce in a blender until smooth (If you prefer a chunkier sauce rather than smooth, then skip this step). Return the sauce to the pan and return to a boil. Add the partially cooked chicken to the pan. Reduce the heat to low, cover the pan with a lid, and leave to simmer for 20 minutes.

5. Season with salt and pepper and stir in the cream and fenugreek leaves. Simmer for another 2-3 minutes.

6. Serve with Basmati rice and/or naan bread and garnish with chopped cilantro or parsley.

Nutritional Value (Amount per Serving):

Calories 327 kcal; Fat 16.3 g; Carbohydrates 18.1 g; Sugar 8.8 g; Protein 27.8 g

LEMON PORK WITH MUSHROOMS

Preparation Time: 15 minutes
Cooking Time: 15 minutes
Serve: 4

Ingredients:

- 1 large egg, lightly beaten
- 1 cup seasoned bread crumbs
- 8 thin boneless pork loin chops (2 ounces each)
- 1/4 teaspoon salt
- 1/8 teaspoon pepper
- 1 tablespoon olive oil
- 1 tablespoon butter
- 1/2 pound sliced fresh mushrooms
- 2 garlic cloves, minced
- 2 teaspoons grated lemon zest
- 1 tablespoon lemon juice
- Lemon wedges, optional

Directions:

1. Separately, place the egg and bread crumbs in small basins. Salt and pepper pork chops; dip in egg, then coat with crumbs, pressing to adhere.

2. Heat the oil in a large skillet over medium heat. Cook the pork in batches until golden brown, about 2-3 minutes per side. Remove from pan and set aside to keep heated.

3. Wipe the pan clean. Melt butter in a pan over medium heat and sauté mushrooms until soft, about 2-3 minutes. Cook and stir for 1 minute after adding the garlic, lemon zest, and lemon juice. Serve with pork. Serve with lemon wedges if preferred.

Nutritional Value (Amount per Serving):

Calories 331 kcal; Fat 15 g; Carbohydrates 19 g; Sugar 2 g; Protein 28 g

Preparation Time: 15 minutes
Cooking Time: 10 minutes
Serve: 12

Ingredients:

- 1 cup plus 1 tablespoon sea salt, divided
- 1 cup sugar
- 1 bone-in pork shoulder butt roast (6 to 8 pounds)
- 1/4 cup barbecue seasoning
- 1/2 teaspoon pepper
- 1/2 cup packed brown sugar
- 12 hamburger buns or kaiser rolls, split

Directions:

1. 1 cup sea salt and 1 cup granulated sugar, combined; spread over all sides of roast. Place in a shallow dish and refrigerate overnight, covered.

2. Preheat the oven to 300 degrees. Scrape the salt and sugar covering from the roast with a kitchen knife; discard any accumulated juices. Place the pork in a large shallow roasting pan. Rub with barbecue spice and season with pepper. Roast for 6-8 hours, or until the meat is tender.

3. Raise the temperature of the oven to 500°. Sprinkle cooked pork with brown sugar and 1 tbsp sea salt. Return the pork to the oven and roast for 10-15 minutes, or until a crisp crust forms. When the meat is cold enough to handle, remove it from the pan and shred it with two forks. Serve hot with fresh buns or rolls.

Nutritional Value (Amount per Serving):

Calories 534 kcal; Fat 24 g; Carbohydrates 33 g; Sugar 14 g; Protein 43g

Preparation Time: 25 minutes
Cooking Time: 8 hours
Serve: 10

Ingredients:

- 1/2 cup reduced-sodium soy sauce
- 1/2 cup water
- 3 tablespoons brown sugar
- 2 tablespoons sesame oil
- 1 tablespoon baking cocoa
- 3 teaspoons chili powder
- 1 garlic clove, minced
- 1/4 teaspoon ground ginger
- 1 boneless pork shoulder butt roast (4-5 pounds)

slaw:

- 3 tablespoons sugar
- 2 tablespoons reduced-sodium soy sauce
- 1 tablespoon Sriracha chili sauce
- 2 teaspoons sesame oil
- 1 teaspoon rice vinegar
- 1 package (14 ounces) coleslaw mix
- 1 tablespoon toasted sesame seeds, optional

assembly:

- 20 flour tortillas (6 inches), warmed
- Optional: Thinly sliced green onions and additional Sriracha chili sauce

Directions:

1. Combine the first 8 ingredients in a mixing bowl. Put the roast in a 6-quart slow cooker. Pour the soy sauce mixture over top. Cook, covered, on low heat for 8-10 hours, or until meat is tender.

2. 1 hour before serving, combine the first 5 slaw ingredients in a mixing bowl. Toss coleslaw mix with dressing and sesame seeds,

if using, in a large mixing basin. Refrigerate, covered, until ready to serve.

3. Remove the roast and remove the fat from the cooking liquids. Return to slow cooker and heat through, shredding the pork with two forks. Serve with slaw in tortillas. Serve with green onions and more chili sauce, if preferred.

Nutritional Value (Amount per Serving):

Calories 603 kcal; Fat 29 g; Carbohydrates 46 g; Sugar 11 g; Protein 37 g

Preparation Time: 15 minutes
Cooking Time: 5 hours
Serve: 8

Ingredients:

- 1 boneless pork shoulder butt roast (3-1/2 to 4 pounds)
- 1 large onion, chopped
- 1 jar (16 ounces) salsa verde
- 2 cans (4 ounces each) chopped green chiles
- 2 teaspoons ground cumin
- 1 teaspoon dried oregano
- 1 teaspoon salt
- 1 teaspoon pepper
- 1/4 teaspoon crushed red pepper flakes
- 1/8 teaspoon ground cinnamon
- 1/4 cup minced fresh cilantro
- Hot cooked grits
- Sour cream, optional

Directions:

1. In a 4-quart slow cooker, combine the pork and onion. Combine salsa, chiles, cumin, oregano, salt, pepper, pepper flakes, and cinnamon in a small bowl; pour over meat. Cook on low for 5-6 hours, or until the meat is soft.

2. Remove the roast and allow it to cool somewhat. Remove the fat from the cooking liquid. Using two forks, shred the pork. Return the pork to the slow cooker and heat thoroughly. Mix in the cilantro. Serve with grits and sour cream, if desired.

Nutritional Value (Amount per Serving):

Calories 349 kcal; Fat 20 g; Carbohydrates 8 g; Sugar 3 g; Protein 34 g

Preparation Time: 15 minutes
Cooking Time: 6 hours
Serve: 8

Ingredients:

- 2 pounds pork tenderloin
- 7 tablespoons stone-ground mustard, divided
- 1 teaspoon pepper, freshly ground
- 1 pound fully cooked boneless ham steak, cut into 1/2-inch cubes
- 1 jar (16 ounces) whole baby dill pickles, undrained, sliced thick
- 2 cups shredded Swiss cheese
- 8 submarine buns, split

Directions:

1. Rub 3 tablespoons mustard over the pork, season with pepper, and set in a 5- or 6-quart slow cooker. Mix in the ham and pickles, including the pickle liquid. Cook on low for 6 hours, or until the potatoes are cooked, flipping halfway through.

2. Using two forks, shred the pork. Sprinkle cheese over meat mixture; cover and simmer for 30 minutes, or until cheese melts.

3. When ready to serve, slice the buns and toast them briefly in a toaster oven or under a broiler. Distribute the remaining mustard evenly on both sides. Top rolls with meat mixture using a slotted spoon. Serve right away.

Nutritional Value (Amount per Serving):

Calories 526 kcal; Fat 20 g; Carbohydrates 36 g; Sugar 4 g; Protein 48 g

Preparation Time: 20 minutes
Cooking Time: 10 minutes
Serve: 4

Ingredients:

- 1/4 cup all-purpose flour
- 1 envelope (1-1/4 ounces) reduced-sodium taco seasoning, divided
- 1-pound boneless pork, cut into 1-1/2x1/8-inch strips
- 2 tablespoons canola oil

piperade:

- 3 tablespoons olive oil
- 1 medium Spanish onion, thinly sliced
- 2 medium sweet red peppers, julienned
- 2 cups canned plum tomatoes, drained (reserve juices)

Directions:

1. Combine flour and half of the spice mix in a small bowl. Toss in the pork, a few pieces at a time, to coat; shake off excess.

2. Heat the canola oil in a large skillet over medium-high heat. Stir-fry the pork for 3-4 minutes, or until it is browned. With a slotted spoon, remove from the pan; cover and keep warm.

3. Warm the olive oil in the same skillet. Stir-fry the onion and peppers until they are crisp-tender. Chop the tomatoes and add them to the skillet. Combine the remaining taco spice and leftover tomato juices in a small bowl. Pour into the skillet. Bring to a boil and continue to cook and stir until thickened. Turn the heat down to medium-low. Return the pork to the skillet and cook thoroughly.

Nutritional Value (Amount per Serving):

Calories 414 kcal; Fat 24 g; Carbohydrates 23 g; Sugar 10 g; Protein 26 g

Preparation Time: 10 minutes
Cooking Time: 3 hours
Serve: 6
Ingredients:

- 6 bone-in pork loin chops (8 ounces each)
- 1/8 teaspoon salt
- Dash pepper
- 1 cup canned cherry pie filling
- 2 teaspoons lemon juice
- 1/2 teaspoon chicken bouillon granules
- 1/8 teaspoon ground mace
- Additional cherry pie filling, warmed, optional

Directions:

1. Brown the pork chops on both sides in a large skillet sprayed with cooking spray over medium heat. Season with salt and pepper to taste.

2. In a 3-quart. Combine pie filling, lemon juice, bouillon, and mace in a slow cooker. Add the pork chops. Cook on low for 3-4 hours, or until the meat is no longer pink. If desired, top with extra pie filling.

Nutritional Value (Amount per Serving):

Calories 371 kcal; Fat 18 g; Carbohydrates 13 g; Sugar 0 g; Protein 36 g

Preparation Time: 10 minutes
Cooking Time: 5 hours
Serve: 6
Ingredients:

- 6 bone-in pork loin chops (8 ounces each)
- 1 tablespoon canola oil
- 1 package (30 ounces) frozen shredded hash brown potatoes, thawed
- 1-1/2 cups shredded cheddar cheese, divided
- 1 can (10-3/4 ounces) condensed cream of celery soup, undiluted
- 1/2 cup whole milk
- 1/2 cup sour cream
- 1/2 teaspoon seasoned salt
- 1/8 teaspoon pepper
- 1 can (2.8 ounces) French-fried onions, divided

Directions:

1. Brown the chops in oil on both sides in a large skillet; set aside. Combine the potatoes, 1 cup cheese, soup, milk, sour cream, seasoned salt, and pepper in a large mixing dish. Add half of the onions and mix well.

2. Top with pork chops in a greased 5-quart slow cooker. Cook on low for 5-6 hours, or until the meat is soft. Finish with the remaining cheese and onions. Cook for another 15 minutes, or until the cheese has melted.

Nutritional Value (Amount per Serving):

Calories 621 kcal; Fat 32 g; Carbohydrates 37 g; Sugar 3 g; Protein 43 g

Preparation Time: 5 minutes
Cooking Time: 25 minutes
Serve: 4

Ingredients:

- 2 tablespoons canola oil, divided
- 1 pork tenderloin (1 pound), cut in half
- 3 tablespoons honey mustard
- 2 medium apples, thinly sliced
- 1 large onion, halved and thinly sliced
- 1/2 cup white wine or apple cider
- 1/8 teaspoon salt
- 1/8 teaspoon pepper

Directions:

1. Preheat the oven to 425° F. 1 tablespoon oil, heated in an ovenproof skillet over medium-high heat Remove tenderloin halves from pan after browning on all sides. Spread mustard on the pork and bake in the oven for 15-20 minutes, or until a thermometer reads 145°.

2. Meanwhile, in a separate skillet, heat the remaining oil over medium heat and sauté the apples and onion for 7 minutes. Bring to a boil with the wine. Reduce heat to low and cook, uncovered, for 5-8 minutes, or until apples and onion are soft. Season with salt and pepper to taste.

3. Remove the pork from the oven and set aside for 5 minutes before slicing. With the apple mixture, serve.

Nutritional Value (Amount per Serving):

Calories 294kcal; Fat 12 g; Carbohydrates 20 g; Sugar 13 g; Protein 24 g

Preparation Time: 5 minutes
Cooking Time: 25 minutes
Serve: 4

Ingredients:

- 1 pork tenderloin (1 pound), cut into 1-inch cubes
- 1 teaspoon all-purpose flour
- 4 teaspoons paprika
- 3/4 teaspoon salt
- 1/4 teaspoon pepper
- 1 tablespoon butter
- 3/4 cup heavy whipping cream
- Hot cooked egg noodles or rice
- Minced fresh parsley, optional

Directions:

1. Flour and seasonings should be mixed into the pork. Melt butter in a large skillet over medium heat; sauté pork until gently browned, about 4-5 minutes.

2. Bring cream to a boil, stirring to dislodge browned pieces from the pan. Cook, uncovered, for 5-7 minutes, or until the cream is slightly thickened.

3. Serve over noodles. Sprinkle with parsley if desired.

Nutritional Value (Amount per Serving):

Calories 323 kcal; Fat 23 g; Carbohydrates 3 g; Sugar 1 g; Protein 24 g

BEEF IN MUSHROOM SAUCE

Preparation Time: 5 minutes
Cooking Time: 20 minutes
Serve: 2

Ingredients:

- 4 tablespoons butter, divided
- 1 teaspoon canola oil
- 2 beef tenderloin steaks (1 inch thick and 4 ounces each)
- 1 cup sliced fresh mushrooms
- 1 tablespoon chopped green onion
- 1 tablespoon all-purpose flour
- 1/8 teaspoon salt
- Dash pepper
- 2/3 cup chicken or beef broth
- 1/8 teaspoon browning sauce, optional

Directions:

1. 2 tablespoons butter and oil in a large skillet over medium-high heat; cook steaks to desired doneness (medium-rare, 135°; medium, 140°), 5-6 minutes per side. Remove from pan, keeping drippings, and set aside to keep warm.

2. In the same pan, cook the drippings and remaining butter over medium-high heat until the mushrooms and green onion are soft. Stir in the flour, salt, and pepper until well combined; gradually add the broth and, if preferred, the browning sauce. Bring to a boil, stirring constantly, and continue to simmer and stir until thickened, about 1-2 minutes. Serve alongside steaks.

Nutritional Value (Amount per Serving):

Calories 417 kcal; Fat 32 g; Carbohydrates 5 g; Sugar 1 g; Protein 26 g

Preparation Time: 10 minutes
Cooking Time: 20 minutes
Serve: 8
Ingredients:

- 2 pounds ground beef
- 1 large onion, finely chopped
- 1 can (20 ounces) pineapple chunks, undrained
- 1 can (16 ounces) kidney beans, rinsed and drained
- 1 can (15-3/4 ounces) pork and beans
- 1 cup ketchup
- 1/4 cup packed brown sugar
- 1/4 cup white vinegar

Directions:

1. Cook the beef and onion in a Dutch oven over medium heat until the meat is no longer pink; drain.

2. Combine the remaining ingredients in a mixing bowl. Bring the water to a boil. Reduce heat to low, cover, and cook for 20 minutes, or until well cooked.

Nutritional Value (Amount per Serving):

Calories 371 kcal; Fat 11 g; Carbohydrates 44 g; Sugar 23 g; Protein 27 g

Preparation Time: 5 minutes
Cooking Time: 25 minutes
Serve: 4

Ingredients:

- 1-1/2 pounds ground beef
- 1 medium onion, chopped
- 2 garlic cloves, minced
- 1/2 cup water
- 1 envelope taco seasoning
- 2 cups shredded cheddar cheese, divided
- 3 cups leftover or refrigerated mashed potatoes, warmed

Directions:

1. Pre-heat the broiler. Cook beef, onion, and garlic in a large ovenproof skillet over medium heat until beef is no longer pink, breaking up beef into crumbles; drain. Heat thoroughly after adding the water and taco seasoning. 1 cup cheese, stirred in Turn off the heat.

2. Mash potatoes and remaining cheese in a basin; spread over beef mixture. Broil 4-6 inches from the heat for 5-6 minutes, or until the top is golden brown.

Nutritional Value (Amount per Serving):

Calories 782 kcal; Fat 45 g; Carbohydrates 40 g; Sugar 5 g; Protein 52 g

Preparation Time: 5 minutes
Cooking Time: 25 minutes
Serve: 8

Ingredients:

- 1 pound ground beef
- 3 garlic cloves, minced
- 2 cartons (32 ounces each) reduced-sodium beef broth
- 2 cans (14-1/2 ounces each) diced tomatoes with green pepper, celery and onion, undrained
- 1 teaspoon dried basil
- 1/2 teaspoon pepper
- 1/2 teaspoon dried oregano
- 1/4 teaspoon salt
- 3 cups uncooked bow tie pasta
- 4 cups fresh spinach, coarsely chopped
- Grated Parmesan cheese

Directions:

1. Cook beef and garlic in a 6-quart stockpot over medium heat until beef is no longer pink, 6-8 minutes; crumble beef; drain. Bring broth, tomatoes, and seasonings to a boil. Return to a boil after adding the pasta. Cook, uncovered, for 7-9 minutes, or until pasta is cooked.

2. Stir in the spinach until it is wilted. Serve with cheese on top.

Nutritional Value (Amount per Serving):

Calories 258 kcal; Fat 7 g; Carbohydrates 30 g; Sugar 8 g; Protein 17 g

Preparation Time: 5 minutes
Cooking Time: 25 minutes
Serve: 4

Ingredients:

- 1 pound beef top sirloin steak, cut into 1-inch cubes
- 6 tablespoons sesame ginger salad dressing, divided
- 1 tablespoon reduced-sodium soy sauce
- 2 cups chopped fresh pineapple
- 2 medium apples, chopped
- 1 tablespoon sweet chili sauce
- 1 tablespoon lime juice
- 1/4 teaspoon pepper
- 1 tablespoon sesame seeds, toasted

Directions:

1. Toss beef with 3 tablespoons dressing and soy sauce in a mixing basin; set aside for 10 minutes. Meanwhile, toss pineapple, apples, chilli sauce, lime juice, and pepper in a large mixing bowl.

2. Thread steak onto four moistened wooden or metal skewers; remove excess marinade. Grill kabobs, covered, over medium heat for 7-9 minutes, rotating occasionally; brush generously with remaining dressing during the last 3 minutes. Sesame seeds are optional. With the pineapple combination, serve.

Nutritional Value (Amount per Serving):

Calories 311 kcal; Fat 11 g; Carbohydrates 28 g; Sugar 21 g; Protein 25 g

Preparation Time: 15 minutes
Cooking Time: 15 minutes
Serve: 8

Ingredients:

- 3 cups all-purpose flour
- 1/2 cup cornmeal
- 1 teaspoon salt
- 1 package (1/4 ounce) quick-rise yeast
- 2 cups warm water (120° to 130°), divided
- 1 tablespoon honey
- 1 pound ground beef
- 1 envelope taco seasoning
- 1 cup refried beans
- 1/3 cup taco sauce
- 2 cups shredded Colby-Monterey Jack cheese

optional toppings:

- Shredded lettuce
- Chopped tomatoes
- Crushed tortilla chips
- Sliced ripe olives, drained
- Diced avocado
- Sour cream
- Salsa

Directions:

1. Preheat the oven to 400 degrees. 2 1/2 cups flour, cornmeal, salt, and yeast 1-1/4 cup warm water and honey in another bowl Gradually add the dry ingredients, mixing only until moistened. Mix in enough of the remaining flour to make a soft dough. Do not knead the dough. Cover and set aside for 20 minutes.

2. Meanwhile, in a small skillet over medium heat, cook and stir beef until no longer pink, breaking meat; drain. Mix in the taco

spice and the remaining water. Cook and stir for 2 minutes, or until the sauce thickens.

3. Form the dough into a 13x9-inch baking pan that has been buttered. Spread beans and taco sauce over dough. Serve with the beef mixture and cheese on top. Bake for 15-18 minutes on a lower oven rack, or until the crust is brown and the cheese has melted. Allow to stand for 5 minutes. Serve with optional garnishes if desired.

Nutritional Value (Amount per Serving):

Calories 469kcal; Fat 16g; Carbohydrates 55 g; Sugar 3 g; Protein 23 g

Preparation Time: 15 minutes
Cooking Time: 15minutes
Serve: 4

Ingredients:

- 1/4 cup balsamic vinegar
- 1/4 cup olive oil
- 2 teaspoons lemon juice
- 1 teaspoon minced fresh thyme or 1/4 teaspoon dried thyme
- 1/4 teaspoon salt
- 1/8 teaspoon coarsely ground pepper
- 1 beef flat iron steak or top sirloin steak (3/4 pound)
- 1 package (9 ounces) ready-to-serve salad greens
- 8 cherry tomatoes, halved
- 4 radishes, sliced
- 1/2 medium ripe avocado, peeled and thinly sliced
- 1/4 cup dried cranberries
- Crumbled blue cheese and additional pepper, optional

Directions:

1. Whisk together the first six ingredients for the dressing. In a resealable plastic bag, combine steak and 1/4 cup dressing; close bag and turn to coat. Refrigerate for at least 8 hours or overnight. Keep the remaining dressing covered and refrigerated until ready to use.

2. Drain the beef, reserving the marinade. 6-8 minutes per side, grill covered over medium heat or broil 4 in. from fire until meat reaches desired doneness (for medium-rare, a thermometer should read 135°; medium, 160°). Allow to stand for 5 minutes before slicing.

3. Divide salad greens among four dishes to serve. Top with steak, tomatoes, radishes, and avocado, garnish with cranberries,

cheese, and pepper, if preferred. Serve with the remaining dressing.

Nutritional Value (Amount per Serving):

Calories 321 kcal; Fat 22 g; Carbohydrates 15 g; Sugar 9 g; Protein 18 g

Preparation Time: 5 minutes
Cooking Time: 25 minutes
Serve: 8
Ingredients:

- 1 package (16 ounces) penne pasta
- 1 pound ground beef
- 1/4 cup butter, cubed
- 1/2 cup all-purpose flour
- 2 cups 2% milk
- 1-1/4 cups beef broth
- 1 tablespoon Worcestershire sauce
- 3 teaspoons ground mustard
- 2 cans (14-1/2 ounces each) diced tomatoes, drained
- 4 green onions, chopped
- 3 cups shredded Colby-Monterey Jack cheese, divided
- 2/3 cup grated Parmesan cheese, divided

Directions:

1. Cook the pasta according to the package directions, then drain.

2. Meanwhile, sauté beef in a Dutch oven over medium heat until no longer pink, 5-7 minutes, crumble beef. Using a slotted spoon, remove from pan and pour off drippings.

3. Melt butter in the same pan over low heat; whisk in flour until smooth. Cook and stir for 2-3 minutes, or until gently browned (do not burn). Whisk in the milk, broth, Worcestershire sauce, and mustard gradually. Bring to a boil, stirring constantly, and continue to simmer and stir until thickened, about 1-2 minutes. Return to a boil after adding the tomatoes. Reduce heat to low and cover for 5 minutes.

4. Heat through the green onions, pasta, and meat. Add half of the cheeses and stir until melted. Garnish with the remaining cheese; cover it and wait till cheese melted.

Nutritional Value (Amount per Serving):

Calories 616 kcal; Fat 29 g; Carbohydrates 56 g; Sugar 7 g; Protein 33 g

Preparation Time: 5 minutes
Cooking Time: 20 minutes
Serve: 4

Ingredients:

- 1 beef top sirloin steak (1 pound), cut into thin strips
- 3 tablespoons reduced-sodium soy sauce
- 1 garlic clove, minced
- 1/4 teaspoon pepper
- 2 tablespoons vegetable oil, divided
- 1 large sweet onion, halved and sliced
- 1 medium green pepper, cut into thin strips
- 1 medium sweet red pepper, cut into thin strips
- 1/4 cup barbecue sauce
- 3 cups hot cooked brown rice

Directions:

1. Toss the meat in a bowl with the soy sauce, garlic, and pepper. In a large nonstick skillet over medium-high heat, heat 1 tablespoon oil. Stir in the meat mixture for 2-3 minutes, or until the beef is browned. Take out of the pan.

2. Add the remaining 1 tablespoon of oil to the pan. Stir-fry the vegetables for 3-4 minutes, or until crisp-tender. Heat through the beef and barbecue sauce. Serve over rice.

Nutritional Value (Amount per Serving):

Calories 387 kcal; Fat 6 g; Carbohydrates 51 g; Sugar 12 g; Protein 30 g

Preparation Time: 5 minutes
Cooking Time: 25 minutes
Serve: 6
Ingredients:

- 2 large eggs, lightly beaten
- 1/4 cup milk
- 1/4 cup ketchup
- 1/2 cup crushed cornflakes
- 4 tablespoons dried minced onion
- 1 teaspoon prepared mustard
- 1 teaspoon salt
- 1/4 teaspoon pepper
- 2 pounds lean ground beef (90% lean)
- Additional ketchup, optional

Directions:

1. Combine the first eight ingredients in a large mixing bowl. Crumble the beef over the mixture and thoroughly mix it in.

2. Fill 12 muffin cups with foil or grease them. Bake for 25 minutes at 350°F, or until a thermometer reads 160°F. Before serving, drain the pasta. If desired, drizzle with ketchup.

Nutritional Value (Amount per Serving):

Calories 301 kcal; Fat 13 g; Carbohydrates 11 g; Sugar 4 g; Protein 32 g

BAKED COD AND ASPARAGUS

Preparation Time: 5 minutes
Cooking Time: 25 minutes
Serve: 4
Ingredients:

- 4 cod fillets (4 ounces each)
- 1-pound fresh thin asparagus, trimmed
- 1 pint cherry tomatoes, halved
- 2 tablespoons lemon juice
- 1-1/2 teaspoons grated lemon zest
- 1/4 cup grated Romano cheese

Directions:

1. Preheat the oven to 375° F. Place the fish and asparagus in a 15x10x1-inch baking pan that has been coated with oil. Place the tomatoes, cut sides down, in a bowl. Brush the fish with lemon juice and garnish with lemon zest. Romano cheese should be sprinkled over the fish and vegetables. Bake for 12 minutes, or until the fish begins to flake easily with a fork.

2. Preheat the broiler after removing the pan from the oven. Broil the cod mixture 3-4 inches from the fire for 2-3 minutes, or until the veggies are gently browned.

Nutritional Value (Amount per Serving):

Calories 141 kcal; Fat 3 g; Carbohydrates 6 g; Sugar 3 g; Protein 23 g

Preparation Time: 5 minutes
Cooking Time: 25 minutes
Serve: 4

Ingredients:

- 1 tablespoon canola oil
- 4 salmon fillets (6 ounces each)
- 1 teaspoon Italian seasoning
- 1/4 teaspoon salt
- 1/2 cup reduced-fat plain yogurt
- 1/4 cup reduced-fat mayonnaise
- 1/4 cup finely chopped cucumber
- 1 teaspoon snipped fresh dill

Directions:

1. Heat the oil in a large skillet over medium-high heat. Season the fish with salt and Italian seasoning. Place the skin side down in the skillet. Turn the heat down to medium. Cook for 5 minutes on each side, or until the salmon begins to flake easily with a fork.

2. Meanwhile, combine the yoghurt, mayonnaise, cucumber, and dill in a small bowl. Serve with grilled salmon.

Nutritional Value (Amount per Serving):

Calories 366 kcal; Fat 25 g; Carbohydrates 4g; Sugar 3 g; Protein 31 g

Preparation Time: 5 minutes
Cooking Time: 10 minutes
Serve: 4

Ingredients:

- 3 tablespoons reduced-fat mayonnaise
- 3 tablespoons grated Parmesan cheese, divided
- 2 teaspoons mustard seed
- 1/4 teaspoon pepper
- 4 sole fillets (6 ounces each)
- 1 cup soft bread crumbs
- 1 green onion, finely chopped
- 1/2 teaspoon ground mustard
- 2 teaspoons butter, melted
- Thinly sliced green onions, optional

Directions:

1. Spread the mayonnaise, 2 tablespoons cheese, mustard seed, and pepper over the tops of the fillets. Place on a broiler pan that has been sprayed with cooking spray. Broil 4 inches from the flame for 3-5 minutes, or until the salmon flakes easily with a fork.

2. Meanwhile, combine the bread crumbs, onion, crushed mustard, and remaining cheese in a small bowl; stir in the butter. Spritz topping with cooking spray before spooning over fillets. Broil until golden brown, about 1-2 minutes more. If desired, garnish with green onions.

Nutritional Value (Amount per Serving):

Calories 267 kcal; Fat 10 g; Carbohydrates 8 g; Sugar 1 g; Protein 35 g

Preparation Time: 25 minutes
Cooking Time: 4 hours
Serve: 10
Ingredients:

- 1/4 cup butter, cubed
- 1/2 pound sliced fresh mushrooms
- 1 medium onion, chopped
- 1 medium sweet pepper, chopped
- 1 teaspoon salt, divided
- 1 teaspoon pepper, divided
- 2 garlic cloves, minced
- 1/4 cup all-purpose flour
- 2 cups reduced-sodium chicken broth
- 2 cups half-and-half cream
- 4 cups uncooked egg noodles (about 6 ounces)
- 3 cans (5 ounces each) light tuna in water, drained
- 2 tablespoons lemon juice
- 2 cups shredded Monterey Jack cheese
- 2 cups frozen peas, thawed
- 2 cups crushed potato chips

Directions:

1. Melt butter in a large skillet over medium-high heat. Cook and stir until the mushrooms, onion, sweet pepper, 1/2 teaspoon salt, and 1/2 teaspoon pepper are soft, 6-8 minutes. Cook for 1 minute more after adding the garlic. Mix in the flour until well combined. Whisk in the broth gradually. Bring to a boil, stirring constantly, and continue to simmer and stir until thickened, about 1-2 minutes.

2. Place in a 5-quart slow cooker. Mix in the cream and noodles. Cook, covered, over low heat for 4-5 hours, or until noodles are

soft. Meanwhile, combine the tuna, lemon juice, and remaining salt and pepper in a small bowl.

3. Remove the insert from the slow cooker. Incorporate the cheese, tuna mixture, and peas into the noodle mixture. Allow to stand for 20 minutes, uncovered. Sprinkle with parsley just before serving.

Nutritional Value (Amount per Serving):

Calories 393 kcal; Fat 21 g; Carbohydrates 28 g; Sugar 5 g; Protein 22 g

Preparation Time: 60 minutes
Cooking Time: 20 minutes
Serve: 10
Ingredients:

- 20 fresh large quahog clams (about 10 pounds)
- 1-pound hot chourico or linguica (smoked Portuguese sausage) or fully cooked Spanish chorizo
- 1 large onion, chopped (about 2 cups)
- 3 teaspoons seafood seasoning
- 1 package (14 ounces) herb stuffing cubes
- 1 cup water
- Optional: Lemon wedges and hot pepper sauce

Directions:

1. In a stockpot, add 2 inches of water. Bring the clams and chourico to a boil. Steam for 15-20 minutes, or until the clams open.

2. Remove the clams and sausage from the pot, reserving 2 cups of the cooking liquid; set aside to cool somewhat. Unopened clams should be discarded.

3. Preheat the oven to 350oF. Remove the clam meat from the shells. Separate the shells and set aside 30 half-shells for stuffing. Put the clam meat in a food processor and pulse until finely minced. Transfer to a large mixing bowl.

4. Remove the casings from the sausage and cut it into 1-1/2-inch pieces. Place all ingredients in a food processor and pulse until finely chopped. Chop the clams and mix in the sausage, onion, and seafood spice. Mix in the stuffing cubes. Add the reserved cooking liquid and enough water to reach the desired consistency.

5. Fill saved shells with clam mixture. Bake in 15x10x1-inch baking dishes. Bake for 15-20 minutes, or until thoroughly heated. Pre-heat the broiler.

6. Broil clams for 4-5 minutes at 4-6 inches from the fire, or until golden brown. Serve with lemon wedges and pepper sauce, if desired.

Nutritional Value (Amount per Serving):

Calories 296 kcal; Fat 11 g; Carbohydrates 34 g; Sugar 3 g; Protein 18 g

Preparation Time: 5 minutes
Cooking Time: 20 minutes
Serve: 4

Ingredients:

- 1 tablespoon canola oil
- 1 small onion, chopped
- 1/4 cup pine nuts
- 1-pound uncooked shrimp (16-20 per pound), peeled and deveined
- 1 cup uncooked pearl (Israeli) couscous
- 2 tablespoons lemon juice
- 3 teaspoons Moroccan seasoning (ras el hanout)
- 1 teaspoon garlic salt
- 2 cups hot water
- Minced fresh parsley, optional

Directions:

1. Heat oil in a large skillet over medium-high heat; sauté onion and pine nuts until onion is translucent, about 2-3 minutes. Stir in the remaining ingredients, except the parsley, and bring to a boil. Reduce heat to low and cover for 4-6 minutes, or until shrimp turn pink.

2. Remove from heat and let aside for 5 minutes. Garnish with parsley if desired.

Nutritional Value (Amount per Serving):

Calories 335 kcal; Fat 11 g; Carbohydrates 34 g; Sugar 1 g; Protein 24 g

Preparation Time: 10 minutes
Cooking Time: 30 minutes
Serve: 2
Ingredients:

- 2 tablespoons mustard seed
- 2 tablespoons celery seed
- 1 tablespoon dill seed
- 1 tablespoon coriander seeds
- 1 tablespoon whole allspice
- 1/2 teaspoon whole cloves
- 4 bay leaves
- 8 quarts water
- 1/4 cup salt
- 1/4 cup lemon juice
- 1 teaspoon cayenne pepper
- 2 whole live Dungeness crabs (2 pounds each)
- Melted butter and lemon wedges

Directions:

1. Place the first seven ingredients on a double layer of cheesecloth. Gather the corners of the fabric to surround the seasonings; bind with string.

2. Bring water, salt, lemon juice, cayenne pepper, and spice bag to a boil in a large stockpot. Return crab to stockpot with tongs; bring to a boil. Reduce heat to low and cover for 15 minutes, or until shells turn bright red.

3. Remove the crab from the saucepan with tongs. Submerge in ice water or run under chilly water. Serve with lemon wedges and melted butter.

Nutritional Value (Amount per Serving):

Calories 245 kcal; Fat 3 g; Carbohydrates 2 g; Sugar 0 g; Protein 50 g

Preparation Time: 5 minutes
Cooking Time: 15 minutes
Serve: 6

Ingredients:

- 2 tablespoons olive oil
- 1 envelope pesto sauce mix
- 1 tablespoon lemon juice
- 6 halibut fillets (4 ounces each)

Directions:

1. Preheat the oven to 450 degrees. Combine the oil, sauce mix, and lemon juice in a small bowl, brush over both sides of the fillets. Place in a 13x9-inch oiled baking dish.

2. 12-15 minutes, uncovered, until the fish begins to flake easily with a fork.

Nutritional Value (Amount per Serving):

Calories 188 kcal; Fat 7 g; Carbohydrates 5 g; Sugar 2 g; Protein 24 g

Preparation Time: 5 minutes
Cooking Time: 20 minutes
Serve: 4

Ingredients:

- 3 to 4 garlic cloves, minced
- 1/4 cup butter, cubed
- 1/4 cup olive oil
- 1-pound uncooked medium shrimp, peeled and deveined
- 1/4 cup lemon juice
- 1/2 teaspoon pepper
- 1/4 teaspoon dried oregano
- 1/2 cup grated Belgioioso Parmesan Cheese
- 1/4 cup dry bread crumbs
- 1/4 cup minced fresh parsley
- Hot cooked angel hair pasta

Directions:

1. Sauté garlic in butter and oil in a 10-inch ovenproof skillet until fragrant. Cook and whisk in the shrimp, lemon juice, pepper, and oregano until the shrimp become pink. Cheese, bread crumbs, and parsley should be sprinkled on top.

2. Broil for 2-3 minutes, or until the topping is golden brown, 6 inches from the flame. Serve with spaghetti.

Nutritional Value (Amount per Serving):

Calories 395 kcal; Fat 30 g; Carbohydrates 9 g; Sugar 1 g; Protein 24 g

Preparation Time: 20 minutes
Cooking Time: 35 minutes
Serve: 6

Ingredients:

- 6 fresh or frozen lobster tails (4 to 5 ounces each), thawed
- 3 tablespoons olive oil
- 1 jalapeno pepper, seeded and minced
- 3 garlic cloves, minced
- 1 can (28 ounces) whole plum tomatoes, undrained
- 1/2 cup julienned soft sun-dried tomatoes (not packed in oil)
- 1/2 cup dry red wine
- 1 teaspoon sugar
- 2 teaspoons salt-free Italian herb seasoning
- 1/2 teaspoon smoked paprika, optional
- 1/4 teaspoon salt
- 1/8 teaspoon pepper
- 1 tablespoon red wine vinegar
- 2 tablespoons butter
- 3 tablespoons finely chopped shallots
- Hot cooked linguine and minced fresh parsley

Directions:

1. Cut through the bottom of the lobster tail lengthwise down the centre using kitchen scissors. Place the lobster tail on a cutting board, cut side up. Cut through the lobster meat and shell with a chef's knife. Remove the meat from the shell with care and chop it into 1-inch pieces. Set aside the lobster shells.

2. Heat the oil in a 6-quart stockpot over medium-high heat. Cook and stir for 1-2 minutes, or until the jalapeno is tender. Cook for 1 minute more after adding the garlic.

3. Break up tomatoes with a spoon and add tomatoes, dried tomatoes, wine, sugar, and seasonings. Mix in the reserved

lobster shells. Bring the water to a boil. Reduce heat to low and cook, covered, for 25-30 minutes, stirring periodically. Set aside the shells. Mix in the vinegar.

4. Melt butter in a large skillet over medium-high heat. Cook, stirring constantly, until the shallots are tender. Cook and stir for 2-4 minutes, or until the lobster meat is opaque. Mix into the tomato mixture. Bring the water to a boil. Reduce heat to low and cook, uncovered, for 2-3 minutes, or until meat is firm but tender.

5. Fill lobster shells with tomato mixture and serve. Serve with linguine and garnish with parsley.

Nutritional Value (Amount per Serving):

Calories 254 kcal; Fat 11 g; Carbohydrates 12 g; Sugar 7 g; Protein 20 g

CUCUMBER WITH DILL

Preparation Time: 20 minutes
Cooking Time: 0 minutes
Serve: 6
Ingredients:

- 2 medium cucumbers, sliced 1/8 inch thick
- 1 tablespoon kosher salt
- 1/2 cup white vinegar
- 1/4 cup snipped fresh dill
- 3 tablespoons sugar
- 1/2 teaspoon coarsely ground pepper

Directions:

1. Place cucumber slices in a colander over a plate and mix with salt. Allow it stand for 15 minutes, stirring once during that time. Rinse and drain well.

2. Combine the vinegar, dill, sugar, and pepper in a large mixing basin. Toss in the cucumbers to coat. Refrigerate for at least 15 minutes before serving, covered.

Nutritional Value (Amount per Serving):

Calories 35 kcal; Fat 0 g; Carbohydrates 8 g; Sugar 7 g; Protein 1 g

Preparation Time: 5 minutes
Cooking Time: 25 minutes
Serve: 12

Ingredients:

- 4 pounds red potatoes, quartered
- 2 teaspoons chicken bouillon granules
- 1 carton (8 ounces) spreadable chive and onion cream cheese
- 1/2 cup half-and-half cream
- 1/4 cup butter, cubed
- 1 teaspoon salt
- 1/4 teaspoon pepper
- Chopped chives, optional

Directions:

1. In a Dutch oven, combine the potatoes and bouillon, then cover with 8 cups water. Bring the water to a boil. Reduce heat to low, cover, and simmer until vegetables are soft, about 15-20 minutes.

2. Return to the pan after draining. Potatoes mashed with cream cheese, cream, butter, salt, and pepper Garnish with chives if desired.

Nutritional Value (Amount per Serving):

Calories 219 kcal; Fat 11 g; Carbohydrates 26 g; Sugar 3 g; Protein 5 g

Preparation Time: 5 minutes
Cooking Time: 20 minutes
Serve: 12
Ingredients:

- 2 pounds fresh baby carrots
- 1/2 cup butter, cubed
- 1/2 cup packed brown sugar
- 2 envelopes ranch salad dressing mix
- Minced fresh parsley, optional

Directions:

1. In a saucepan, combine carrots and 1 inch of water. Bring the water to a boil. Reduce heat to medium-low, cover, and simmer for 8-10 minutes, or until crisp-tender. Set aside after draining.

2. In the same pan, whisk together the butter, brown sugar, and salad dressing mix until smooth. Mix in the carrots. Cook and stir for 5 minutes over medium heat, or until glazed. If desired, garnish with parsley.

Nutritional Value (Amount per Serving):

Calories 156 kcal; Fat 8 g; Carbohydrates 22 g; Sugar 13 g; Protein 1 g

Preparation Time: 5 minutes
Cooking Time: 25 minutes
Serve: 12

Ingredients:

- 3 large yellow onions, sliced
- 3 tablespoons butter
- 6 large tart red apples, sliced
- 1/2 cup packed brown sugar
- 1 teaspoon salt
- 1/2 teaspoon paprika
- 1/8 teaspoon ground nutmeg

Directions:

1. Sauté onions in butter in a large cast-iron or other heavy skillet until soft. Place the apples on top of the onions. Combine the remaining ingredients and sprinkle on top of the apples.

2. Simmer for 10 minutes, covered. Uncover and continue to cook for 5 minutes more, or until the apples are soft. Use a slotted spoon to serve.

Nutritional Value (Amount per Serving):

Calories 137 kcal; Fat 3 g; Carbohydrates 28 g; Sugar 24 g; Protein 1 g

Preparation Time: 10 minutes
Cooking Time: 0 minutes
Serve: 6

Ingredients:

- 4 cups frozen peas (about 16 ounces), thawed
- 1/2 cup shredded sharp cheddar cheese
- 1/2 cup ranch salad dressing
- 1/3 cup chopped red onion
- 1/4 teaspoon salt
- 1/4 teaspoon pepper
- 4 bacon strips, cooked and crumbled

Directions:

1. Toss the first 6 ingredients together to coat. Refrigerate for at least 30 minutes, covered. Before serving, toss in the bacon.

Nutritional Value (Amount per Serving):

Calories 218 kcal; Fat 14 g; Carbohydrates 14 g; Sugar 6 g; Protein 9 g

Preparation Time: 15 minutes
Cooking Time: 0 minutes
Serve: 6

Ingredients:

- 1 quart cherry tomatoes, halved
- 1/4 cup canola oil
- 3 tablespoons white vinegar
- 1/2 teaspoon salt
- 1/2 teaspoon sugar
- 1/4 cup minced fresh parsley
- 1 to 2 teaspoons minced fresh basil
- 1 to 2 teaspoons minced fresh oregano

Directions:

1. In a small bowl, place the tomatoes. In a small mixing bowl, combine the oil, vinegar, salt, and sugar; toss in the herbs. Pour over tomatoes and toss lightly to coat. Refrigerate overnight, covered.

Nutritional Value (Amount per Serving):

Calories 103 kcal; Fat 10 g; Carbohydrates 4 g; Sugar 3 g; Protein 1 g

Preparation Time: 10 minutes
Cooking Time: 15 minutes
Serve: 8

Ingredients:

- 1 tube (8 ounces) refrigerated crescent rolls
- 6 bacon strips, cooked and crumbled
- 1 teaspoon onion powder

Directions:

1. Make eight triangles out of the crescent dough. 1 tablespoon bacon, set aside Sprinkle the remaining bacon and onion powder over the triangles; wrap up and set point side down on an oiled baking sheet. Garnish with reserved bacon.

2. Bake at 375°F for 10-15 minutes, or until golden brown. Serve hot.

Nutritional Value (Amount per Serving):

Calories 140 kcal; Fat 5 g; Carbohydrates 11 g; Sugar 2 g; Protein 3 g

Preparation Time: 20 minutes
Cooking Time: 10 minutes
Serve: 4

Ingredients:

- 1 large zucchini, quartered and sliced
- 1 large carrot, chopped
- 1 tablespoon butter
- 2 cups reduced-sodium chicken broth
- 1 cup quick-cooking barley
- 2 green onions, chopped
- 1/2 teaspoon dried marjoram
- 1/4 teaspoon salt
- 1/8 teaspoon pepper

Directions:

1. Sauté zucchini and carrot in butter in a large pot until crisp-tender. Bring the broth to a boil. Stir in the barley. Reduce heat to low, cover, and cook for 10-12 minutes, or until barley is soft.

2. Combine the onions, marjoram, salt, and pepper in a mixing bowl. Remove from the heat and let aside for 5 minutes, covered.

Nutritional Value (Amount per Serving):

Calories 219 kcal; Fat 4 g; Carbohydrates 39 g; Sugar 3 g; Protein 9 g

Preparation Time: 15 minutes
Cooking Time: 0 minutes
Serve: 6

Ingredients:

- 2 cups all-purpose flour
- 4 large eggs, lightly beaten
- 1/3 cup 2% milk
- 2 teaspoons salt
- 8 cups water
- 1 tablespoon butter
- Minced fresh parsley, optional

Directions:

1. In a large mixing basin, whisk together the flour, eggs, milk, and salt until smooth (dough will be sticky). Bring water to a boil in a large saucepan over high heat. Place the dough in a colander or spaetzle maker that has been sprayed with cooking spray and set it over boiling water.

2. Press the dough with a wooden spoon until little bits drop into the hot water. Cook for 2 minutes, or until the dumplings are soft and float to the surface. Toss with butter after removing with a slotted spoon. Sprinkle with parsley if desired.

Nutritional Value (Amount per Serving):

Calories 223 kcal; Fat 6 g; Carbohydrates 33 g; Sugar 1 g; Protein 9 g

Preparation Time: 10 minutes
Cooking Time: 0 minutes
Serve: 2

Ingredients:

- 1 snack-sized cup (4 ounces) pineapple tidbits
- 1/3 cup chopped apple
- 1/3 cup cubed cantaloupe
- 10 green grapes, halved
- 6 fresh strawberries, quartered
- 1 medium kiwifruit, peeled and sliced

Dressing:

- 2 tablespoons mayonnaise
- 2 tablespoons sour cream
- 1-1/2 teaspoons sugar
- 1 teaspoon orange juice
- 1/4 teaspoon lemon juice
- 1/4 teaspoon grated lemon or orange zest

Directions:

1. Drain the pineapple, keeping 1 teaspoon of the juice. Combine the pineapple, apple, cantaloupe, grapes, strawberries, and kiwi in a salad dish. Combine the dressing ingredients in a small bowl; add the reserved pineapple juice and stir thoroughly. Refrigerate the fruit and dressing until completely cooled. Pour dressing over fruit and toss to coat just before serving.

Nutritional Value (Amount per Serving):

Calories 136 kcal; Fat 2 g; Carbohydrates 28 g; Sugar 22 g; Protein 3 g

You can plan your meals with these easy dinner recipes. The nicest part about easy weeknight dinner dishes is that you can plan what you'll eat. You can plan dinner for the entire week because there are so many recipes. You may spend less time in the kitchen this way. By using these easy weeknight dinner recipes, you will have an opportunity to make meals in your home. These easy dinner recipes are time-saving, and you do not have to worry about spending an entire evening making dinner for you and your family. This also implies that you won't be tempted to consume your meals outside.

Printed in Great Britain
by Amazon